Hiking In
Zion National Park

THE TRAILS

Published by the Zion Natural History Association

ACKNOWLEDGMENTS

This book is a consolidation and reorganization of information from several sources, including Roland Wauer's *A Guide to the Trails of Zion National Park,* which has been revised many times with input from numerous persons. Another prime source, especially for mileages, was the unpublished draft *Exploring the Backcountry of Zion National Park* by Thomas Brereton and James Dunaway. Lynn Bickerton, from England, spent the winter working in Zion as a volunteer and re-drew the maps.

Additional information came from National Park Service employees, visitors, and landowners adjacent to the park. The final product was made possible with the backing of the Zion Natural History Association and the efforts of Companion Press. Thanks to all!

- Bob Lineback

All photographs are from the Zion National Park files. Color photos by: Tom Brereton (cover, 22 bottom, 27) Brian Chan (21, 23, 24, 25 top, 26 top) J. L. Crawford (22 top) and James Dunaway (25 bottom, 28).

Publication Coordinator: Jamie Gentry

ISBN 0-915630-24-9
Second printing, 1991

Produced by Companion Press
Santa Barbara, California
Edited by Jane Freeburg
Designed by Lucy Brown

Printed on Recycled Paper

Title page: Walters Wiggles, ingenious switchbacks on the trail to Scout Lookout.

Welcome to Zion National Park! This park had its beginning in 1909 as Mukuntuweap National Monument and has been expanded several times to encompass outstanding natural features found nowhere else in the world. While some of these features can be viewed from roads, many can only be experienced from trails. This is as it should be — parks are meant to be preserved with minimum impact from people, while allowing us to come in close contact with the natural world.

Every year about 2 million visitors from this country and around the world come to Zion; about 60 percent or more walk on a trail somewhere in the park. Each visitor inherits a responsibility to leave the park unimpaired for those who follow. Parks can only survive in our busy world if people feel strongly enough to take care of them.

We invite you to go for a walk in your park. Go safely, go lightly on the land. Each day you spend here will enrich your life.

> Harold L. Grafe
> Park Superintendent
> 1981-1991

CONTENTS

While the information in this book was correct at publication, conditions change. It is the hiker's responsibility to acquire permission to cross private property to either access or egress park lands. Please check at a visitor center regarding the latest access information when crossing private property.

HIKING WITH MINIMUM IMPACT

Zion National Park is an extraordinary resource offering the hiker a diversity of experience opportunities. The 147,000-acre Park, with elevations ranging from 3,640 to 8,726 feet, supports a wide assortment of plant and animal life in a rich environment of brilliantly-hued canyons, isolated mesas and etched terraces of slickrock.

Zion's Backcountry Zones: The spectrum of wilderness experience

Not all people need or seek the same experiences in the backcountry. Zion offers choices within three use zone categories. **Trail Zones** are the most commonly visited and easily accessible areas. Frontcountry trails are near main paved roadways. Backcountry trails are further from the road, and often involve overnight backpacking. Hikers who prefer off-trail hiking in regularly-traveled wilderness areas might choose **Primitive Route Zones.** The greatest opportunities for solitude and primitive wilderness are found in **Crosscountry Zones,** where travel is on the terms of the rugged terrain; higher levels of expertise, physical conditioning and preparation are necessary.

Your hiking trip in Zion National Park will be most enjoyable if you *plan* to make it a safe one. Let a friend or relative know your trip plan and expected return time so they can inform park rangers if you do not return. *Rescue* is not a sure or immediate service; be prepared to survive on your own. Enjoy the beauty and freedom of Zion's backcountry. With freedom comes the responsibility to take care of the land, and to leave without signs of your passing. This also reduces the need for additional regulations. Minimum impact principles are an investment in the future integrity of the wilderness. Be it tomorrow or in years to come, let those that follow you have the opportunity to experience a natural Zion National Park.

Appreciate the Sensitivity of the World Around You: Allowing Survival

Zion is a land where only pockets of opportunity — the mesa tops and sheltered side canyons — seem to escape nature's harsh influence. Vegetation that can survive the extremes in temperatures and soil moisture here can be described as "hardy" — but once disturbed, restoration can be a matter of decades.

Above the narrow canyon creek beds are **sandy benches** formed by water and wind deposited soils. The plants that hold these structures in fragile stability are easily disturbed by foot traffic. Slumping can occur with slight disturbance — rutting develops with repeated use. Hike in the flood plain when possible. If you must cross a bench, tread on lesser slopes and pre-existing paths; avoid stepping on vegetation.

In some areas of the park, particularly in the pinyon-juniper woodland, a community association of lichen and moss grows on the soil, forming a dark, spongy surface called **cryptogamic soil**. These fragile areas resist erosion, absorb moisture and offer favorable sites for the sprouting of plants. Stay on trails, rock, or barren ground where possible — take special care to avoid cryptogamic soils if you can. Small, isolated plant communities, called **hanging gardens**, grow at seeps on the canyon walls. Throughout the summer, the delicate green fronds of the ferns are a backdrop to the blossoms of monkey flower, shooting star, columbine and cardinal flower. These unique habitat areas provide a home to the **Zion Snail** — found nowhere else in the world. **As with all things in the park, please look and enjoy, but do not touch or disturb.**

The Minimum Impact Ethic: Think About What You do

Backcountry travel in Zion does make an impact on this vulnerable, sensitive environment. In everything you do —

whether choosing a route, selecting a campsite, or enjoying your camp—there is potential long-term influence.

Stay on trails where they are available; do not shortcut. Avoid or tread lightly in unique and sensitive ecosystems. The survival or destruction of these resources hinges more on your attitude and action than on any list of regulations.

Campsite Selection

Permits are required for all overnight trips. "No Camping" areas are posted on visitor center maps; these are generally near roads, trailheads, day use areas, or park inholdings. Always camp away from and out of sight of the trail. Camp at least 100 feet from any water source (although in narrow canyons this may be impossible). Camping ¼ mile or more away from springs spreads impacts and allows wildlife to drink unhindered by your presence. Avoid making campsite improvements or disturbing even dead vegetation. Do not construct benches, tables, rock or log shelters, or bough beds. If you find items like these, please dismantle and scatter the items so the area looks natural again.

In *desert areas,* choose previously-used campsites or areas of bare soil to localize impact. In *plateau areas*, where ecosystems are more tolerant of use and frost heaving helps eliminate soil compaction, select a campsite that has not been recently occupied, thus spreading out use and allowing natural recovery. In *narrow canyon areas*, when weather is cloudy or rain is forecast, select a safe site above the high water mark. Go lightly on the benches to prevent hard-to-erase impacts. Avoid vegetation and unstable soils, and direct your activities to sandbars along the river when it is safe.

No open fires are allowed in the Zion backcountry. Campfire impacts are unacceptable — scarring, soil sterilization, loss of humus source materials, and vegetation damage from firewood gathering . Carry a backpacking stove, or plan simple, lightweight "no cook" meals as experienced desert hikers do.

If you carry it in, carry it out. Leave nothing behind or buried, not even food scraps or grease. Help remove litter that other hikers may have dropped. Leave the backcountry wilder and cleaner than when you entered.

Although you may never intentionally feed wildlife, many backcountry campers contribute to wildlife problems by failing to secure their food while they sleep. Skunks, ringtail cats, squirrels, pack rats and other rodents have been known to graw through nylon materials or expensive backpacks. When you make camp for the night, assume these critters live in the vicinity. If you leave equipment items with food smells on the ground, these small animals will probably get into them. To avoid this, look around your camp carefully and suspend your pack or foodsack a few feet off the ground by hanging it with a short cord from a tree branch or stick.

Avoiding Other Impacts

Pets are not allowed away from the roadways or in the backcountry. No matter how well behaved or harmless, pets are a disruption to wildlife patterns and other visitors. Pet kennel service is available in St. George or Cedar City.

Human waste must be buried more than 100 feet (preferably 1/4 mile or more) from water sources, trails or campsites. Dig a hole 6 to 8 inches deep, choosing a spot with dark, rich soil which assists decomposition. Carry out toilet paper — a zip-type plastic bag is a good trash carrier. Leave as little evidence of the hole as you can.

Water should be boiled, treated or filtered before drinking. Surface waters may be contaminated with giardia, a protozoan, or bacteria that can cause serious illness and intestinal problems. Carry water at least 100 feet away from the water source to wash dishes, clothes or yourself — using biodegradable soap.

Groups of more than 12 people must be broken into smaller, separately traveling parties (6 or less is encouraged.) Large groups cause greater impacts and diminish the experience of others.

Bicycles and other vehicles are not allowed off the roadways in Zion. Even the tracks of mountain bikes leave unacceptable imprints on the soil. Wilderness is a place where man's machines are intentionally left behind to maintain the primitive experience.

Firearms, electric generators, and chainsaws are not allowed in the backcountry at any time. Thoughtful backcountry hikers do not go down the trail yelling and screaming. Many people enjoy the quiet of the backcountry. Wildlife viewing opportunities increase in the absence of manmade noise.

Taking Care of Yourself:
Recognizing Hazards and Minimizing Risks

Can one enjoy the wilderness without being consumed by its rigors? The key to safe backcountry travel is to take the time to recognize the hazard, calculate the risk, and control the threat. Think!

Physical fitness increases your chance of a safe backcountry trip. Traveling in an unfit or overextended condition increases the chances of having an accident. Plan for the severity of the terrain, take your time, and adjust the pace to the slowest member of your group.

Take the proper **equipment**, a good map, and adequate amounts of food and water. When selecting equipment, take only what is necessary and choose the lightest alternative. In summer, wear light-colored clothing, a hat, and sunscreen. In cooler seasons, prepare for rain and snow. Carry enough food and water to last beyond your planned return, in case of backcountry delays. Always carry first aid supplies.

Acrophobia — Fear of Heights: If you have a fear of heights, you may want to avoid certain trails with immediately adjacent vertical exposures. These include Angels Landing, the West Rim Trail below West Rim Spring, Observation Point, Hidden Canyon, and the Canyon Overlook Trail.

Desert Travel: During summer, when traveling between unknown water sources, carry at least one gallon of water per person per day — and drink it. Heed your body's message when you are thirsty. When you sweat a lot, you should increase your electrolyte intake by drinking fruit juice or including extra salts and sugars in your diet. Be aware of the signs and first aid treatment for heat cramps and heat exhaustion.

Plateau Areas: Anticipate cooler temperatures and possibly rain (snow in the spring or fall). During thunderstorms, minimize lightning danger by avoiding exposed canyon rims and high points. Do not take shelter under lone trees.

Canyon Hikes: Zion's narrow canyons are subject to sudden, unexpected flashflooding. Hiking in these areas requires additional information (see Important Narrows Information, p. 18). Much of this information applies to other narrow canyon hikes in the Zion area.

Horses: Zion has just minor use by horses, compared to some western national parks. If you happen to meet some horses along the trail, give them the right of way. Get off the trail and stand quietly while the stock passes. Don't let things blow or flap on your pack, startling the animals.

Rattlesnakes: Rattlesnakes are relatively rare. You can avoid them by paying attention to what's on the ground wherever you walk in the park. If you go climbing or scrambling, check before placing your hand on ledges or in places where reptiles could be.

Other Tips: Keep back from cliff edges. They can be unstable or slippery. Don't roll or throw rocks, which accelerates erosion and destroys vegetation. People may be hurt below you. Wade or swim only where it is safe; watch out for submerged objects or tricky river currents.

Zion Seasons: Spring and fall's moderate temperatures are pleasant times for hiking in Zion. In spring, snow run-off will eliminate narrow canyon hiking. In winter, snow and ice conditions close many of Zion's higher elevation backcountry trails, but lower areas are always accessible. Summer high temperatures in Zion Canyon usually fluctuate around 100°F. If thunderstorms are absent, summer is a good time for hiking the narrow, shaded canyons. The higher plateaus may also be pleasant when it is hot at the lower elevations.

Fishing: Because of regular sediment flushing during flashfloods, fishing is generally poor in the streams and creeks found in Zion. A Utah Fishing License is required if you want to fish in the park.

Insects: Almost all locations in Zion have periods when certain insects can be pesty. Deerflies can be common along creeks in early summer, and seem attracted to legs — the best defense is to wear long pants. If it's hot, try wearing pants wet to make hiking cooler.

Tiny gnats called "no see ums" can be particularly irritating in late spring and early summer in certain areas. The worst outbreaks last about two weeks at any elevation, with the dates varying from season to season. "No see ums" fly about the face and bite the delicate skin around the eyes, neck, or behind the ears. Some people are more sensitive than others to these insects. Various commercial lotions seem to work effectively against "no see ums."

Mosquitoes can be bothersome at night in several areas of the park during the summer months. The best defense is a tent with a tight screen door, or repellent.

Shuttle Service: Shuttle service to trailheads is provided for a fee by a park concessioner; contact Zion Lodge or the visitor centers for information.

Publications and Hiker Information

Backcountry permits, topographic maps, publications on hiking trails and backcountry routes, and general interest publications are available at the Zion Canyon and Kolob Canyons Visitor Centers. The National Park Service provides free handouts on horse use, rock climbing, and winter snow use.

Management: How you can help

Zion National Park is a natural area, thus focusing management on the preservation of biologic and physical features found in this area. The National Park Service manages the backcountry of Zion with two basic goals: 1) to protect and preserve park resources so that they are available for future generations; 2) to assure visitors the opportunity for a quality experience. Zion National Park is developing a backcountry management plan to outline policies and procedures that park management will use to implement identified objectives. The plan will be a public document; a statement of long-range management goals. It will also provide strategy and working guidelines for the park staff to use in daily operations.

What can you do to help preserve Zion?

Report any adverse impacts or activities destructive to your park that you see during your trip. Remembering details will help the Park Service investigate the problem. If you see cattle or other livestock on NPS land, please report it. The area has a long history of livestock grazing which management is trying to eliminate on park lands.

Trail **register boxes** are found throughout the park. The purpose of these registers is to help measure backcountry impacts by monitoring the number of people using different areas.

Lightning-caused **fires** occur during the summer on the plateaus of Zion. Under certain conditions beneficial to the ecosystem they are allowed to burn. During fire danger periods most fires are discovered by surveillance from the fire lookout or from observation planes. If you witness a wildfire that is not being monitored, please report it. Don't risk your safety by trying to put it out yourself.

Zion National Park is managed by the National Park Service, U.S. Department of the Interior. If you have any suggestions or comments about the Zion backcountry, please direct them to:

Superintendent
Zion National Park • Springdale, UT 84767 • (801) 772-3256

GUIDE TO HIKING IN ZION

All hike ratings are subjective, but the following general "type hike" evaluations used in this book may help guide you to a hike of your choice.

Easy walks are perfect if you have limited time or don't want anything too strenuous. These are well maintained trails.

Short hikes can be completed in 2-3 hours or less if you hike fast. Take water and comfortable footwear.

Moderate hikes take about a half-day for most people, and may be quite strenuous depending on the terrain. Take a small day pack with water, snacks, and first aid materials. Wear hiking footwear.

Long hikes are full day or overnight hikes. Be prepared for changing weather conditions; take food, water and gear to ensure your comfort and survival.

Longer Trail Hiking Trips

Zion is a relatively small national park, with diverse topography dividing it into several geographic and ecologic areas. A hiker wishing a long, multi-day trip could instead consider several two-day hikes in different backcountry areas. In springtime, for example, hikers could take two days in the Petrified Forest-Coalpits area, then drive to Kolob Canyons for 2-3 days in the La Verkin Creek area.

Hikers that don't want to interrupt their hike with a car shuttle may consider connecting hikes together. This usually involves crossing or walking adjacent to park roads for short distances. Some longer hikes are summarized below:

East entrance to Lee Pass: 49.5 miles. This hike involves walking adjacent to Zion Canyon Scenic Drive from Weeping Rock to Grotto Picnic Area.

Lee Pass to Grotto Picnic Area: 37.5 miles. Follow the La Verkin Creek and Hop Valley Trails to the Hop Valley Trailhead. From there, follow the Connector Trail for 4 miles to the Wildcat Canyon Trail; follow this to the West Rim Trail and descend that to the Grotto Picnic Area.

Lava Point to East Entrance: 27 miles, see above.

ZION CANYON TRAILS

Beautiful Zion Canyon is known worldwide for its striking cliffs above the erosive Virgin River. After a stop at the Zion Canyon Visitor Center to begin learning about Zion, the visitor will discover trails that match a variety of hiking levels. Trails are clearly marked on the map/brochure available at entrance stations and visitor centers. Most trails are open year-round, although ice or snow may close sections of trail for periods during the winter months. On hot summer days, hike in early morning or late afternoon, avoiding the mid-day heat. Zion Canyon is usually less crowded at these times and the lighting provides better photographs. Zion Canyon is a popular day use area; there is no camping except in the developed campgrounds near the South Entrance.

THE COURT OF THE PATRIARCHS

An *easy* concrete trail of only 50 yards, this trail is a popular stop for visitors year-round. The viewpoint at the end of the trail provides views of the Streaked Wall, the Sentinel, Court of the Patriarchs, Mt. Moroni, the Spearhead, and Angels Landing. To the east of the viewpoint (above you) are Mountain of the Sun and the Twin Brothers.

Trail Head

The trail is accessed from the parking area 2.2 miles up the Zion Canyon Scenic Drive.

THE SAND BENCH TRAIL

Trail Head

Accessed from the Court of the Patriarchs Parking Area, the trail begins across the road and leads to the footbridge crossing the Virgin River. The trail is a *moderate* 1.9 miles with a steep climb onto the pinyon-juniper covered plateau. A loop trip on this sand bench gives a different perspective of the views seen from Court of the Patriarchs. Allow about 3 hours round trip; the trail can be used all year, but is hot and dusty in summer. This trail is heavily used by the park horseback concessionaire from spring through fall; stand quietly off the trail when riders are passing. The section of trail from the Virgin River to Birch Creek is poorly delineated; make sure you bring a map.

THE EMERALD POOLS TRAIL SYSTEM

	Lower Pool	Upper Pool
Type Hike:	easy walk	short hike
Average Hiking Time:	50 mins.	2 hrs.
		(round trip)

Trail Head

Emerald Pools Parking Area, 2.5 miles up the Zion Canyon Scenic Drive, accesses a trail network leading to exquisite Lower and Upper Emerald Pools. This area is heavily visited most of the year. The .6 mile concrete trail to Lower Emerald Pool is suitable for baby strollers and wheelchairs with assistance. From there a steeper, unpaved trail continues .5 mile to Upper Emerald Pool. The trail to Upper Pool experienced severe flash flood damage during 1987; it is very rough and rocky. The Emerald Pools are formed by a small year-round creek coming out of Heaps Canyon, named after a Mormon pioneer of the 1870s. Two small waterfalls with pools below (Upper and Lower Emerald Pools) are the main attractions. Views include Lady Mountain, the Great White Throne, Red Arch Mountain and other majestic cliffs in all directions.

The pleasant trail to the Lower Pool passes through a small forest community of cottonwood, boxelder and Gambel oak. The upper trails provide a drier habitat with more yucca, cacti and scrub oak in addition to the ever-present pinyon-juniper. From the trail to Upper Pool you can see shaded, more moist north-facing slopes that sustain ponderosa pine and Douglas fir. Fall foliage colors usually peak here in October.

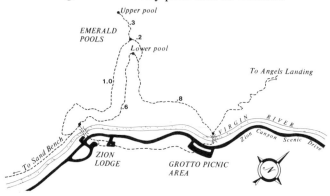

14

Should you wish to hike an alternate loop, an established trail from behind the ice machine at the north end of Zion Lodge leads to Grotto Picnic Area; it parallels the scenic drive, emerging behind the Park Service residence at the south end of Grotto Picnic area. The trail is signed at both ends and has a dirt surface with gentle grades.

Note: You can access the Sand Bench or West Rim Trails from the Emerald Pools Trail system.

Caution: Take care to stay *on* the trails which parallel the top of the cliffs. The trails are marked and safe, but several persons have fallen to their deaths going off-trail to the cliff edge. The cliff edges are unstable, down-sloping, and slippery. Supervise children closely. There are other hikers below; do not drop anything or roll rocks.

THE TRAIL TO SCOUT LOOKOUT AND ROUTE TO ANGELS LANDING

	Scout Lookout	*Angels Landing*
Average Hiking Time:	2½ hrs.	4 hrs.
	(round trip)	

The **moderate** 1.9 mile trail to Scout Lookout is paved, though steep — it climbs 1,000 feet. The route to Angels Landing is more rugged, adding .5 mile and another 500 feet in elevation to the hike. Both trails are popular. The best time to hike here is in spring and fall or on early summer mornings.

Trail Head

The trailhead is located at Grotto Picnic Area, 3.2 miles up the Zion Canyon Scenic Drive. Cross the footbridge over the Virgin River and turn right.

One of the park's construction wonders, this trail was cut into solid rock in 1926, including an amazing series of 21 short switchbacks called "Walters Wiggles." Both Scout Lookout and Angels Landing offer spectacular views over sheer drops into Zion Canyon. From Scout Lookout it is 3 miles of uphill hiking to the West Rim (see p. 39).

Caution: The route to Angels Landing involves travel along a steep, narrow ridge with support chains anchored intermittently along the route. Footing can be slippery even when the rock is dry. Unevenly surfaced steps are cut into the rock with major cliff dropoffs adjacent. Keep off when it is wet, icy, or thunderstorms are in the area. Plan to be off before dark. Younger children should skip this trail; older children must be closely supervised.

THE WEEPING ROCK TRAIL

Trail Head

A paved *easy walk* through mixed forest vegetation leads to a spring seep alcove which nurtures lush vegetation. Continuous rain "weeps" from the ceiling of Weeping Rock above. Weeping Rock is found 4.4 miles up Zion Canyon Scenic Drive. The .2 mile trail takes about 25 minutes round trip, and is too steep for wheelchairs.

This is a popular stop for almost everyone who visits Zion Canyon. Interpretive signs explain the natural history of the area. Ferns and flowers thrive in the wet alcove, and the light rain falling from Weeping Rock feels cool and refreshing on a hot day. Fall colors can be quite striking here.

THE TRAILS TO HIDDEN CANYON AND OBSERVATION POINT

Trail Head

These are *moderate* hikes, usually done separately. The 1.1 mile paved trail to Hidden Canyon is cut into solid rock in places, and climbs 1,000 feet. The 3.7 mile trail to Observation Point climbs 2,200 feet; both are accessed from the Weeping Rock Parking Area and receive moderate use in summer and on spring weekends. It's about a 3 hour round trip to Hidden Canyon; about 6 hours to Observation Point and back. These trails feature slickrock formations, sheer cliffs and narrow canyons. Stay back from cliff edges. They can be unstable or slippery because sand or pebbles act as ballbearings on slickrock.

Hidden Canyon is a water-carved gorge between Cable Mountain and The Great White Throne. The trail ends at the mouth of Hidden Canyon; you may wish to take more time and walk up along the dry stream bed. Grottoes and water-formed features decorate the canyon walls, including a small arch found on the right wall .5 mile upstream from the canyon mouth.

The trail to Observation Point skirts the base of Cable Mountain, then cuts through a cavelike "narrows" and climbs up to the plateau covered with ponderosa pine, Gambel oak and manzanita. The trail ends at an overlook with views of the

Great White Throne, Cable Mountain, the West Rim, Angels Landing and Zion Canyon.

The Observation Point Trail connects with the Echo Canyon Trail, which leads to Deertrap and Cable Mountains, (p. 31) and the East Mesa Trail which leads to the park boundary.

Camping

Camping is allowed along the East Mesa Trail and in upper Echo Canyon.

THE GATEWAY TO THE NARROWS TRAIL

The park's most popular trail follows the pools and small rapids of the Virgin River up the dramatically narrowing canyon. High cliffs and abundant springs offer a cool, moist environment where a diversity of plants and small animals live. In summer many visitors stop and soak their feet in the cool river.

Trail Head

This *easy walk* is constructed of concrete and is usable by baby strollers and wheelchairs with assistance. The 1.0 mile trail begins at the Temple of Sinawava Parking Area at the end of the Zion Canyon Scenic Drive, and takes about 1½ hours to complete. It is a delightful walk during late afternoon or an early summer evening. Near the start of the trail note the "Narrow Canyon Danger Level" sign, updated daily to reflect conditions for river hiking beyond the end of this trail.

Seepage area along the Gateway to the Narrows Trail.

UP THE NARROWS TO ORDERVILLE CANYON

Trail Head

Those who choose this **moderate** hike beyond the paved trail walk a river bottom route (no trail), and will get their feet wet! The Virgin River has carved a chasm 2,000 feet deep into the Markagunt Plateau in Zion National Park. The river meanders through a storm-sculptured gorge of sandstone arches, grottoes, and soaring fluted walls.

On a hot, clear day there are few things more enjoyable than river hiking. Lush riparian vegetation, hanging gardens, "Mystery Falls," the ever-narrowing canyon, and the relaxing sound of running water beckon travelers from around the world to explore the Virgin River Narrows.

It is 1.8 miles from the end of the Gateway to the Narrows Trail to Orderville Canyon — a half-day round trip. (Travel up Orderville Canyon is limited by obstacles which may change with each flood and season.) Many visitors wade up the Virgin River a short way, spending less time.

IMPORTANT NARROWS INFORMATION:

Know the Narrow Canyon Danger Level before hiking up the river.

NARROW CANYON DANGER LEVEL

☐ **Low** — *Forecast calls for favorable conditions. Most people hike the Narrows during these periods. Be prepared for changing conditions.*

☐ **Moderate** — *Possible flashflooding and adverse conditions. Much wading in waist-deep water and some swimming possible.*

☐ **High** — *Travel not recommended. High probability of flashflooding, high river level, and/or cold temperatures. Swimming and continuous wading necessary in strong currents.*

☐ **Extreme** — Closed due to dangerous conditions.

The National Park Service receives a daily site-specific weather forecast in summer and monitors river conditions. The "Danger Level" is posted each day in the visitor centers.

However, *conditions may change rapidly and unexpectedly.* Carefully consider the current danger level and the experience and condition of the weakest hiker in your group before entering the Narrows. Hike with at least one other person.

Wear wool, polypropolene or any synthetic fabric that wicks moisture away from the skin. Comfortable, lightweight (when wet) boots are a must. Take a day pack with survival items for your comfort and safety; be out of the Narrows before the day begins to fade.

Season: The best times to hike the Narrows is during the summer when the weather is clear and stable. Thunderstorms from mid-July through early September can cause dangerous flash floods.

Permits/Restrictions: Permits are not required for short day trips into the Narrows from the end of the Gateway to the Narrows trail. They are required for all long trips from Chamberlain's Ranch — get more information on this hike at a visitor center.

Crossing and Wading the River: Choose crossing and wading spots carefully. Seek shallow areas in slow moving water; level stretches with several channels; or wide places with small ripples all the way across. Be alert to dangers downstream. Do not cross directly above cascades or rough, rocky areas with swift-moving water. Look for alternatives; you can avoid most obstacles and deep spots. Use a *walking stick* as a stable "third leg" during crossings.

Be prepared to swim. Chest-deep holes may occur even when water levels are low. Pack your belongings in sealed plastic bags in your backpack for protection. Early or late season cold water, shade and chilly nights require extra dry, warm clothing to prevent hypothermia.

Flashfloods: Narrow desert canyons are notorious for flashflooding. The North Fork of the Virgin River drains a large watershed; remember, blue sky overhead does not eliminate the possibility of flooding caused by torrents of water from upstream.

As you hike, watch for signs of past floods — water line stains on the rock walls. Look for places where you can climb above this level if you must escape a flood.

Signs of possible flashflooding:
- *Sudden changes in water clarity from translucent to muddy.*
- *Rising water levels or stronger currents.*

- *Build up of thunderclouds or distant sounds of thunder; rainfall.*
- *An increasing roar of water up canyon.*

Seek higher ground if you observe any of these signs. **Do not try to beat a flood out of the canyon.** Stay on safe ground and wait until the flood subsides. Water levels usually drop within 24 hours. If caught by flooding in an area with no escape, try to take shelter behind a jutting fin of rock which can break the force of the initial mass of water and debris. It may be possible to wedge yourself into a crack above water level. Even climbing a few feet may save your life.

Hypothermia: Immersion in cold water or exposure in wet clothing to cool air can cool the body to dangerous levels. Hypothermia may occur quickly without the victim's awareness. Avoid cotton clothing and eat high energy food, especially sugars and starches, before you are chilled. Watch for these signs of hypothermia:

- *Uncontrollable shivering*
- *Stumbling and poor coordination*
- *Confusion or slurred speech*
- *Disorientation*
- *Fatigue and weakness*

If you recognize any of these symptoms, stop hiking and immediately replace wet clothing. Warm the victim with your own body, and a hot drink. A pre-warmed sleeping bag and shelter from breeze will help prevent further heat loss.

THE WATCHMAN TRAIL

Type Hike: Short hike.
Distance, One Way: About 1.5 miles from either trailhead.
Average Hiking Time: About 2 hours round trip.
Season: All year, best during spring and fall.
Use Level: Light.

This trail climbs to a plateau near the base of The Watchman, an impressive crag looming over the southern portion of Zion Canyon. The trail's end viewpoint offers outstanding views of the West Temple, the Towers of the Virgin, and the town of Springdale. The trail passes through

Neagle Ridge, adjacent to the La Verkin Creek Trail.

The Sundial, Altar of Sacrifice and Towers of the Virgin.

The Great White Throne from Scout Lookout area.

Larsen Cabin and Tucupit Point, Middle Fork of Taylor Creek Trail.

Opposite: Beartrap Canyon, below the falls. Accessible from the La Verkin or Willis Creek Trails.
Above: Taylor Creek Headwater Canyons.
Right: Double Arch Alcove, Middle Fork of Taylor Creek Trail.

Above: Headwaters of Timber Creek, Nagunt Mesa.
Right: The Zion Narrows, beyond the Gateway to the Narrows Trail.

Looking south into Hop Valley from the trail.

Heaps Canyon and Zion Canyon, from West Rim Trail.

spring seepage/riparian areas that nurture a variety of plants
and attract wildlife; be alert for birds.

From the Zion Canyon Visitor center, drive south (toward
Springdale) 0.7 mile and turn east (left) at the entrance to
Watchman Campground. Turn left again at the service road
and proceed 0.2 mile to the trailhead. Parking is available here.
A "Watchman Trail" sign indicates the start of the Watchman
Trail.

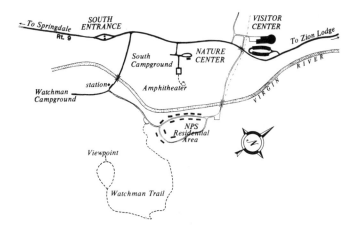

Cautions: Be careful near the cliff edge. Supervise children
closely. Trail may be muddy and slippery after a saturating rain
or winter snow.

EAST SIDE TRAILS

The trails in this section are accessible from the East
Entrance Road. St. Rt. 9 winds eastward and upward as it
leaves Zion Canyon. After exiting the Zion-Mt.Carmel Tunnel
one enters a world of cross-bedded sandstone and weirdly
eroded slickrock topped with the heavily vegetated East Rim
Plateau.

THE CANYON OVERLOOK TRAIL

Type Hike: Easy.
Distance, One Way: .5 mile.
Average Hiking Time: One hour
Season: All year.
Use Level: High.

Trail Head

Interpretive leaflets for this self-guiding trail are available at the Zion Canyon Visitor Center, and usually at the trailhead. The trailside environment, quite different from that of Zion Canyon, features plants and animals surviving in a rock and sand habitat. Pine Creek has formed a convoluted narrow chasm below the trail. The trails-end viewpoint offers views of the West and East Temples, Towers of the Virgin, the Streaked Wall, and other prominent features of lower Zion Canyon. The trail begins at the parking area just beyond the east end of the Zion-Mt. Carmel Tunnel, 5 miles east of the Zion Canyon Visitor Center.

Cautions: A series of uneven steps are cut into the sandstone at the start of this trail, followed by irregular rock and sand surfaces. Supervise children closely near vertical drop-offs.

Angels Landing, from Cable Mountain.

THE TRAILS TO CABLE AND DEERTRAP MOUNTAINS

Type Hike: Long — *from East Entrance an elevation gain of about 800 feet in 5.6 miles. Many hikers depart via the Echo Canyon Trail with its spectacular slickrock (and steep, rough descent) and emerge at Weeping Rock to meet shuttle or ride arrangements. The East Rim is also accessible from Weeping Rock (the first part of the trail is described in the Hidden Canyon/Observation Point section) — a strenuous alternative with an elevation gain of 2,100 feet in 5 miles.*

Distance, One Way:

East Entrance trailhead to Stave Spring Jct . . . . 5.6 mi

Stave Spring Jct to Cable Mountain . . . . 2.9 mi

Stave Spring Jct to Deertrap Mountain . . . . 3.2 mi

Stave Spring Jct to East boundary barricade . . . . 0.9 mi

Stave Spring Jct to Weeping Rock . . . . 5.0 mi

Average Hiking Time: *Many people spend 2-3 days hiking in this area. East Entrance to Weeping Rock makes a long day hike.*
Season: *Late spring or fall are best; summers can be warm.*
Use Levels: *Light.*

Trail Head

The views from Cable and Deertrap Mountains are favorites of many Zion hikers. From Deertrap you can see Court of the Patriarchs, Twin Brothers and the East Temple. The Cable Mountain trail offers views of the hoodoos atop the Great White Throne, the cableworks, Angels Landing, Observation Point and the West Rim. There are excellent views of the massive White Cliffs from the trail above East Entrance. Late spring and summer bring a profusion of wildflowers on the East Rim — some bloom into late summer.

Primary trailhead access is from the East Entrance, 12 miles east of the Zion Canyon Visitor Center. (Backcountry permits are not available at the entrance station.) A drinking water faucet at the entrance station is operational from May to October. About 100 yards west of the entrance station a short road leads north to a gravel parking area, the trailhead.

The East Rim may also be reached from Weeping Rock via the trail to Observation Point.

In fair, dry weather high clearance vehicles may access the East Rim trails via the North Fork County Road. From the East Entrance Station, drive east 2.5 miles on St. Rt. 9. Turn left on the maintained dirt road (to be paved - Spring '88) marked "Navajo Lake". Proceed north 5.4 miles to the Ponderosa Hunting Club; turn left. You are entering private property; respect landowner rights and shut the gate behind you. Proceed past the many side roads about .8 mile. Turn left on Buck Road, then take an immediate right at the next fork. Go .6 mile to the next junction and take the left fork. Continue .1 mile to another fork. Turn right, taking West Pine Street .3 mile west, following signs to the "Gooder-Reagan" cabin. Passing below the A-frame cabin the road becomes much rougher — it is not maintained the last .2 mile to the park boundary. At the park boundary drive through the gate, closing it behind you so cattle cannot enter the park. The trail begins 50 yards further at the barricade.

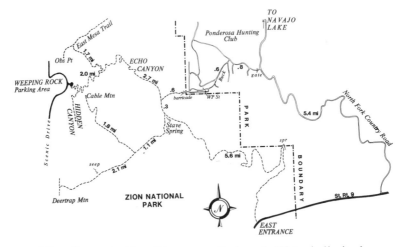

All trails on the East Rim are well signed. Water is limited: check at the Zion Canyon Visitor Center for the current condition of Stave Spring, the primary water source. Another small, unnamed spring is located at the park boundary in Cave Canyon, north of East Entrance. This seep has a small beautiful narrows below it; scramble down to it downstream from the sharp hairpin turn where the trail leaves Cave Canyon. Another unnamed seep can be accessed from the Deertrap Mountain trail in a drainage at the head of Hidden Canyon.

Please do not climb on the Cable Mountain Draw Works. This is all that remains of the cable-tram system once used to lower lumber to the floor of Zion Canyon. This historic structure is a monument to the tenacious pioneer spirit that settled the West.

Camping   Camping is allowed on most of the East Rim Plateau. No camping is allowed on the trails to Hidden Canyon or

Observation Point, or within 1 mile of East Entrance. Do not camp within a quarter mile of Stave Spring; you may disrupt wildlife watering patterns. Camp out of sight of all trails.

There are many beautiful pine groves on the East Rim Plateau, and some magnificent flats on the south end of Deertrap Mountain. Upper Echo Canyon offers some small sandy camping areas .5 mile northeast of the junction with the Observation Point Trail.

SOUTHWEST DESERT AREA

This 12,000 acre corner of Zion National Park has the lowest elevation (3,640 feet) in the park, experiences the warmest temperatures, and gets the most sunshine. As a result it has the most desert-like environment in Zion, with plants and animals adapted to water conserving and heat avoidance lifestyles. Easily accessible from St. Rt. 9 near the town of Rockville, it is quiet and offers a different hiking experience from the rest of Zion. The views of Mt. Kinesava, the West Temple, and Cougar Mountain change dramatically with location and time of day. If you visit Zion during the spring, fall, or winter, consider exploring this delightful area!

Left: Yucca in bloom.
Top: Ringtail cat, a night creature.
Above: Collared lizard.

PETRIFIED FOREST TRAIL

Type Hike: Long. Rolling terrain with little elevation change.
Distance, One Way: *Gate by St. Rt. 9 to park boundary fence
(walk or drive)* . . . . *1.3 mi*
Park boundary gate to Huber Wash . . . . *2.1 mi*
Huber Wash to Scoggins Wash . . . . *1.8 mi*
Scoggins Wash to Old Scoggins Stock Trail (via trail) . . *1.4 mi*
Old Scoggins Stock Trail to Coalpits Wash (via trail) . . . *1.5 mi*
Total mileage in the park: *6.8 mi*
*Petrified Forest Trail to Scoggins Wash via the Old Scoggins
Stock Trail* . . . . *0.3 mi*
Average Hiking Time: *About 5-6 hours from boundary fence to
Coalpits Wash.*
Season: *November-May; avoid this area in summer or after a
heavy rain. Wildflowers best from March-May.*
Use Level: *Light. Off-trail routes in this relatively gentle
terrain make attractive loop trips possible.*

*Trail
Head*

For many hikers, the peace and quiet found in this open
desert is as enticing as the beautiful vistas. Petrified wood is
scattered throughout the area; remember, this is a national park
— you may *not* collect samples.

To reach the trailhead, measure the distance on your vehicle
odometer as you drive south on St. Rt. 9. From the South
Entrance Station drive south 3.5 miles; pull off between
Springdale and Rockville onto a large dirt turnout on the right
(north) side of the road. If the road is muddy or you have a low-
clearance vehicle, park here and begin your hike. Please
respect the private land that this dirt road crosses. High
clearance vehicles may proceed through the gate and drive 1.3
miles to the park boundary. Please close all gates behind you
on this trip. At the park boundary is a locked vehicle gate with
an adjacent horse/hiker gate, the beginning of the Petrified
Forest Trail. If you drove to this point park in one of the dirt
pullouts near the gate.

For .6 mile the trail follows a rough 4-wheel drive road used
to access power lines to Springdale. The trail turns right
(north) at a trail sign. Soon you pass a colorful painted desert

area to the right, followed by the usually-dry Huber Wash and the Petrified Forest.

After a short uphill climb the trail descends into Scoggins Wash, where a tiny stream may run during the spring. The trail makes an abrupt turn to the west as it crosses Scoggins Wash.

After additional gentle climbs and descents the trail passes a sign marking the Old Scoggins Stock Trail, built by pioneers through a break in the cliffs to facilitate movement of their livestock. The Petrified Forest Trail terminates at Coalpits Wash, a reliable creek. You may hike upstream following the creek for another full day of hiking. Other side trips might include explorations to Crater Hill, or into the downstream canyon of Coalpits Wash.

Traveling downstream about 50 yards, the creek crosses the bedrock of the Shinarump formation creating a small, pretty cascade. 100 yards further downstream the creek curves to the left (south) where it has undercut the rock, forming an alcove. At the downstream end of this alcove is a small, reliable spring; note the small but delightful hanging garden.

Camping   There are many desirable places to camp in this section of the park. Camp north of power lines and out of sight of the trail. Be careful not to contaminate the small creeks; camp 100 feet or more away. Some hikers enjoy dry camping on the pinyon-juniper studded plateau of the Petrified Forest. Please pick a previously-used site when possible and leave it cleaner than you found it. Please don't camp at the historic oil well site, a relic from 1908 oil exploration in the area.

May the sounds of coyotes hunting after dark be the only "disturbance" to your nights out here!

Additional Exploring: Make sure you have a topographic map with you and know how to read it. There are numerous off-trail routes that can connect with the Petrified Forest Trail to make loop trips of various lengths.

KOLOB TERRACE TRAILS

The Kolob Terrace area is one of the least known treasures of Zion. This less-developed area is accessible via the paved Kolob Reservoir Road which heads north from the town of Virgin, Utah located on St. Rt. 9, 14 miles west of the South Entrance. A small primitive campground is located near Lava Point Lookout; no water is available. Park inholdings — parcels of privately-owned land — are located within this section of the park. You may see cattle or some cabins adjacent to the road.

And what scenery! Cougar Mountain, the canyons of North Creek, Firepit Knoll, Pine Valley Peak, and the Guardian Angels are just several of the many outstanding features visible from the Kolob Reservoir Road.

THE HOP VALLEY TRAIL

Type Hike: A long hike usually done as an overnight trip. The trail loses almost 1,000 feet as it drops to La Verkin Creek.
Distance, one way: *6.7 miles*
Average Hiking Time: 4-6 hours to La Verkin Creek, longer if you hike the reverse uphill direction.
Season: Spring and fall best; summers are hot.
Use Level: Light, moderate on holidays.
Caution: Purify water before drinking; livestock contamination.

Trail Head

Hop Valley is a favorite access to the La Verkin Creek-Kolob Arch area (see p.46.) While it has a private inholding, this does not detract from the beautiful flat, grassy valley bottom, where a shallow year-round stream meanders between the vertical cliff walls. Cattle may be present on the inholding from June to October. From the town of Virgin, drive north on the Kolob Reservoir Road 13 miles to the "Hop Valley Trail" sign. The trail begins on the north side of the graveled parking area.

The trail leads north, passing west of volcanic Firepit Knoll through sage and cactus flats and Gambel oak groves. Red Butte, a BLM Wilderness Study Area, is prominent to the northwest. The views are worthwhile and the walking easy, but sandy, for about 1.5 miles. After reaching the green hiker gate (the fence marks the start of the inholding) the trail follows a faint, primitive 4-wheel drive road bearing east initially. Please respect this private property as you pass through. Cedar posts have been placed to delineate the way. Stay on the main 4WD road. It soon makes a steep descent of about .4 mile to the bottom of Hop Valley where the track disappears. Head downstream following either the stream or cattle trails. Choose the most direct or convenient route — you may get your feet wet.

You will pass a suspension cable hung across the valley that once supported a cattle fence. Shortly downstream, Langston Canyon enters from the east. Next you will approach another cattle fence that should be intact. During the summer the stream will disappear in this vicinty as the water seeps into the sandy wash. The hiker gate is up on the bench east of the stream. (There should be no cattle north of this fence: if you observe any, notify the Park Service after completing your trip.) Less than .1 mile from the fence the trail crosses the wash one last time, then climbs the hill on the west side of the canyon. Watch for the sign marking the point where the trail leaves the wash.

After cresting the hill, you will make a steep switchbacking descent into the La Verkin Creek valley.

Camping

Camping is allowed north of the cattle fence. There are good sites in the shady pine groves adjacent to the wash. Remember to camp out of sight of the trail. Many hikers continue to La Verkin Creek to camp, although there are fewer opportunities for solitude there.

THE WILDCAT CANYON, CONNECTOR, AND NORTHGATE PEAKS TRAILS

Type Hike: *Moderate; but can be done as an overnight trip. There is a 450-ft elevation gain from the Wildcat Canyon Trailhead to the West Rim Trail; in between is a 500-ft descent into Wildcat Canyon and an equal ascent out of it.*

Distance, one way: *Wildcat Canyon Trail: 5.8 mi; Connector Trail: 4.0 mi; Northgate Peaks Trail Spur: 1.2 mi*

Average Hiking Time: *Half a day. To make a day of it, do both trails and emerge at the West Rim Trailhead to meet shuttle or arranged ride.*

Season: *Spring, summer or fall. The Wildcat Canyon Trail also serves as a cross-country ski route during the winter; check at the visitor center for information.*

Use Level: *Light.*

These trails offer a great variety in plant and wildlife habitats. There are shady ponderosa pine areas, aspen groves, grassy meadows, and Gambel oak thickets. The viewpoint at the end of the Northgate Peaks Trail boasts views of Northgate

Peaks, North Guardian Angel, and the canyons of the Left Fork of North Creek. The Wildcat Canyon Trail offers views of Pocket Mesa, Russell Gulch, the black lava cliffs of the Upper Kolob Plateau, and Wildcat Canyon. The geology of this area contrasts white sandstone with dark basaltic lava flows.

A long wildflower season begins in late spring and continues through the end of summer; fall colors can be spectactular. These trails provide access to a number of cross-country backcountry routes.

The Connector Trail links the Hop Valley Trail with the Wildcat Canyon Trail. This pretty 4 mile trail enables you to do an extended (38 mile) hike in the park (from Lee Pass to the Grotto Picnic Area) without following roads. The Connector Trail begins at the Hop Valley Trailhead and joins the Wildcat Canyon Trail 0.9 mile from the Wildcat Canyon Trailhead.

Trail Head

The Wildcat Canyon Trailhead is 16 miles north of Virgin, Utah on the paved Kolob Reservoir Road; it is well signed. The trail initially passes through upland sage flats among Gambel oak groves northeast of Pine Valley Peak. .7 mile from the trailhead there is a shady pine forest; nearby is a small pothole seep as marked on the topographic map.

The Northgate Peaks Trail is relatively level and ends at a lava outcrop viewpoint. The Wildcat Canyon Trail continues on a steady uphill grade passing Russell Gulch. It crests at a scenic grass-shrub meadow before descending into Wildcat Canyon.

The most reliable spring on this route is located about .4 mile southwest of where the trail crosses Wildcat Canyon. This small, unnamed spring gurgles through a lava rockslide adjacent to the trail; it is clearly marked by a "Purify Water" sign.

As you approach the West Rim Trail you will pass an old piece of farm equipment, a grain drill that was used in the area before it became a park.

At the West Rim Trail Junction either continue south on the West Rim Trail to Zion Canyon (p. 39) or walk north .1 mile to the West Rim Trailhead, with vehicle or foot access to Lava Point.

Camping

Outstanding camp sites may be found off the Northgate Peaks Trail, or near the meadow area on the Wildcat Canyon Trail where there are scenic views. Wildcat Canyon itself, and the small spring, offer little in the way of camping.

THE WEST RIM TRAIL

Type Hike: Long. *Often done as an overnight from the West Rim Trailhead below Lava Point to Grotto Picnic Area — a 3,100-foot loss in elevation. In the reverse direction there is a 5-mile steep ascent to the West Rim.*

Distance, one way: *West Rim Trailhead to Wildcat Canyon Trail Junction* .... *0.1 mi*
Wildcat Canyon Trail Junction to Sawmill Springs Trail Junction .... *0.7 mi*
Sawmill Springs Trail Junction to Potato Hollow *4.3mi*
Potato Hollow to Telephone Canyon Trail Junction *1.3mi*
Telephone Canyon Trail Junction to West Rim Spring Junction (via Rim Route) *3.2mi*
West Rim Spring Junction to Grotto Picnic Area *4.7mi*
West Rim Trail Total (via Rim Route) *14.3mi*

Telephone Canyon Cutoff Trail *1.8mi*
Sawmill Springs Spur Trail .... *0.3 mi*

Average Hiking Time: *Two days. To add to this hike, consider starting at the Wildcat Canyon Trailhead, which adds almost 6 more miles.* *See p. 37.*

Season: *Late spring, summer and fall. A 6 mile cross-country ski trip from the Kolob Reservoir Road is necessary to reach the West Rim in winter.*

Use Level: *This popular backcountry trail receives steady use from spring through fall.*

Many hikers feel the scenic vistas from the West Rim Trail are without equal. Horse Pasture Plateau, with its diverse vegetation and wildlife, is a "peninsula" extending south from Lava Point. Near the vertical edges of the plateau are thousand-foot cliffs; views include Wildcat Canyon, the Left and Right Forks of North Creek, Imlay Canyon, Phantom Valley and the highly eroded Virgin River Narrows area. Peaks include the North and South Guardian Angels, Greatheart Mesa, Mount Majestic and the prominent landmarks of Zion Canyon.

Trail Head

To reach the trailhead from Virgin, Utah, go north on the Kolob Reservoir Road 18 miles until the pavement ends; continue on the maintained gravel road, acceptable for all passenger vehicles. About 21 miles from Virgin turn right at the sign to Lava Point. In 1.0 mile there is another signed juction.

If the road is dry, turn left toward the West Rim Trailhead which is 1.3 miles further. (Even 4-wheel drive vehicles can have difficulty getting back up this road if it is muddy.) If the road is wet or snowy, turn right at the junction and proceed .6 mile to Lava Point Campground. Near site 3 "Barneys Trail" is marked by a small sign. This .3 mile connector trail leads down to the road to the West Rim Trailhead which is .8 mile from the campground.

Other trailhead options include starting at the Wildcat Canyon Trailhead (p. 37) or at Grotto Picnic Area (p. 15).

Water: As in other areas of the park, water is a limiting factor for the hiker. Purify all natural water. Three signed springs can usually be relied upon:

1) Sawmill Springs is found in a small meadow valley by taking a .3 mile spur trail. The small pond may dry up; about 20 yards north is a circular metal barrel cover over the spring. Replace it after taking your water.

2) Potato Hollow is a lush meadow area with a small "cattle pond" constructed during ranching days. An intermittent spring feeds the pond.

3) West Rim Spring is reached by a 100-yard trail from the junction of the Telephone Canyon, Rim Route and Grotto Picnic Area Trails. A pipe provides water from the seepage area.

Starting at the West Rim Trailhead, the trail is level and rolling until it descends into Potato Hollow. After a moderate hill it skirts Sleepy Hollow, climbs to Telephone Canyon Junction.

Lightning strikes frequently on Horse Pasture Plateau. An uncontrolled wildfire burned through this area in 1980 destroying most of the vegetation. Years of fire protection allowed fuels to accumulate unnaturally; firefighters were unable to suppress the fire for several days. Catastrophic fires of this type were rare when frequent natural burning occurred — before pioneers came to the area and began suppressing all fires.

If you have time, walk east about 1 mile to the scene of another lightning-caused fire that burned about 250 acres

The canyons of the Right Fork of North Creek, from the West Rim Trail.

during the summer of 1987. This fire was monitored and allowed to burn under prescribed conditions, with the goals of brush removal and habitat restoration. Note the large number of trees that survived this fire.

The Rim Route from Telephone Canyon Trail Junction is relatively level until the south tip of Horse Pasture Plateau; there the trail descends to West Rim Spring Junction. The Telephone Canyon Trail, a shortcut, descends just past the junction then becomes fairly level to West Rim Spring Junction.

From West Rim Spring Junction the trail descends steeply adjacent to a vertical cliff. Much of the last five miles of the trail are pavement, rock, or concrete. 3 miles from West Rim Spring Junction you will come to Scout Lookout where the route to Angels Landing begins (p. 15). Always stay back from cliff edges. They may be unstable or slippery due to gravel and loose sand.

Camping The West Rim Trail is the most popular overnight hike in the park; minimize your impact. Camp away from the trail, choosing a little-used place for your site, and do not alter or damage any vegetation. Camp 1/4 mile or more from the heavily-used Potato Hollow and West Rim Spring areas. About 1.5 miles down the trail from West Rim Spring is a footbridge over a narrow drainage; there is no camping from this point to Grotto Picnic Area.

THE WILLIS CREEK TRAIL

Type Hike: Long; total elevation loss is 2,300 feet.
Distance, One Way: 7.5 miles to Beartrap Canyon.
Average Hiking Time: 5-7 hours. Most hikers take 2-4 days to fully explore the La Verkin Creek (p. 46) and Hop Valley areas. (p. 36)
Season: Summer and fall. Crossing the Spilsbury land is not advised during the Utah State Deer Hunt; check at the visitor centers for exact dates.
Use Levels: Very light. This is a prime area for solitude and quiet.

Trail
Head

The La Verkin and Willis Creek Canyons remind many hikers of the Virgin River Narrows — with less water and more easily negotiated. Deciduous and evergreen trees are plentiful, providing ample shade for pleasant summer hiking. The 1,000-foot vertical canyon walls are very impressive. There are spectacular views of the Kolob area from the Spilsbury land.

Side canyons can lead to interesting explorations. Leaving the trail, one may hike into the La Verkin Creek Wilderness Study Area (BLM). Beartrap Canyon is one of the jewels of Zion.

To reach the trailhead from Virgin, Utah, drive north on the Kolob Reservoir Road 26 miles. Just past the small inlet stream on the north side of Kolob Reservoir, make an immediate left (south) turn at the sign reading "Thank You For Visiting Kolob Reservoir." This dirt road is not maintained; if recent rain or snow has made the road muddy, leave your vehicle here to avoid getting stuck.

Under dry conditions, drive down the dirt road 1.2 miles, ignoring any lesser roads that branch off. As you near the end of the Indian Hollow arm of Kolob Reservoir, look for a wire gate and a sign reading "To La Verkin Creek in Zion NP" to your right in an aspen grove. Vehicles are not allowed beyond this point. Park in the aspen grove; do not block the sign, roadway, or gate. As you pass through the private Spilsbury property to reach Zion National Park, respect landowner rights by leaving all gates as you find them. Avoid disturbing cattle, and pass straight through this area as your pace allows.

The trail follows ranch roads for 4 miles; they show less use further from the trailhead. Read your topographic map to avoid confusion; there are more dirt roads than shown on the map. Plastic flagging has been tied periodically along the correct route.

2.7 miles downhill from the trailhead gate are a fence and open gate bordering the large meadow area of Birch Spring, one of the sources of Willis Creek. Stay on the dirt road as it skirts the north side of the meadow with the old cabins in it. The road reaches the west side of the meadow and curves south as it passes through another fence. About 100 yards west of this fence you must leave this road; watch for flagging. Go south, following faint vehicle tracks through this smaller dry meadow until it joins another little-used dirt road which heads west. This road becomes easier to follow, descends, then makes a sharp bend to the south and begins descending steeply. Before long it turns into a trail. Follow it to the park boundary gate. Shut the gate behind you to keep cattle out of the park. The trail levels out when it reaches the pine forest area where the various Willis Creek headwater drainages come together.

The trail is not clearly defined from here to Hop Valley — it crosses the creek many times. Getting your feet wet is unavoidable. You can't get lost; there are massive cliff walls on each side. Although walking may be more difficult than on more well-maintained trails, this is a delightful route.

Falls in Beartrap Canyon

Get water in the upper section of Willis Creek — it is often dry downstream until you reach the confluence with La Verkin Creek, a reliable stream with occasional springs along it.

Don't miss Beartrap Canyon. The shallow springfed stream, green vegetation, and red rock are charming. It's an easy .3 mile walk up to the waterfall; to go beyond the falls safely you need technical climbing gear.

Camping

There are numerous campsites in the Willis Creek headwaters area. For small parties, there are other sites along the way; one large site is found at the confluence of Willis and La Verkin Creeks. As the canyon widens downstream from Beartrap Canyon there are more campsites. There is no camping on the Spilsbury property.

KOLOB CANYONS TRAILS

The Finger Canyons of the Kolob exhibit some of the finest scenery on earth. The massive stone cliffs, colored a brilliant red, form cathedral-like vistas on the grandest scale. Most visitors to Zion never see the Kolob Canyons, even though they are easily accessed from the Kolob Canyons Exit #40 off I-15, 17 miles south of Cedar City, Utah.

It takes about one hour to drive from Zion Canyon to the Kolob Canyons. A new visitor center was constructed here in 1984 by the Zion Natural History Association and donated to the National Park Service. Park personnel are available to answer questions, sell maps and books, and issue free backcountry permits.

Hiking the two developed trails in this area can be very rewarding.

Timber Top and Gregory Butte

THE MIDDLE FORK OF TAYLOR CREEK TRAIL

Type Hike: Moderate; elevation gain just over 400 ft.

Distance, one way: 2.7 miles to Double Arch Alcove.

Average Hiking Time: About 4 hours, round trip.

Season: Spring, summer, fall — fall colors can be spectacular. Trail muddy after a rainstorm or winter snow.

Use Levels: Light; moderate use on holiday weekends or at peak times.

Trail Head

Camping

This is a pleasant walk along a little creek beneath the imposing cliffs of Tucupit and Paria Points looming 1,500 feet or more above. The natural history of the area is fascinating, with diverse plant and animal habitats and interesting geology as you travel up the canyon. The trail ends at Double Arch Alcove, where the lower slope is covered with a delicate layer of golden columbine.

From the Kolob Canyons Visitor Center, drive east on the paved Kolob Canyons Road 2 miles to the signed Taylor Creek Trail Parking Area. The trail immediately descends to parallel Taylor Creek, sometimes crossing it, sometimes shortcutting benches beside it.

The historic Larsen Cabin is located just west of the confluence of the forks of Taylor Creek. The North Fork is to the left; the Middle Fork continues straight ahead.

Entering the canyon of the Middle Fork, the trail becomes rougher as its route is dictated by the terrain. Watch for the beaten path as you travel upstream; try to stay on the main route. Too much off-trail hiking will give this canyon a "worn" appearance.

After passing the old Fife Cabin, the canyon makes a bend to the right, arriving at Double Arch Alcove, a large colorful grotto with a high arch above.

This is a day use area with no camping permitted. If you wish to camp nearby, get a permit to go up the North Fork of Taylor Creek.

THE LA VERKIN CREEK AND KOLOB ARCH TRAILS

Type Hike: Long. *Visiting the arch usually involves a two-day trip — longer to explore further or to relax and enjoy the area. There is an 800-foot elevation loss from Lee Pass to Kolob Arch Junction. The spur trail to Kolob Arch Viewpoint is rocky and more primitive.*

Distance, One Way: Lee Pass to "Corral" *4.8mi*
"Corral" to Kolob Arch Trail Junction *1.8mi*
Kolob Arch Trail Junction to Kolob Arch Viewpoint . . . . *0.6 mi*
Kolob Arch Trail Junction to Hop Valley Trail . . . . *0.3 mi*
Hop Valley Trail to Beartrap Canyon *1.9mi*

Average Hiking Time: 4-6 hours to Kolob Arch Trail Junction; *longer to hike out, as it is uphill. Many use the Hop Valley (p. 36) or Willis Creek (p. 42) access routes also.*

Season: All year; best in spring or fall. Avoid this hike when snow is melting or after a saturating rain.

Use Levels: A popular backpacking area, especially during peak visitation periods such as Memorial Day, Easter, college spring break and Labor Day.

Cautions: Purify all water, as the headwaters area is heavily used by sheep and cattle. Some years snowmelt runoff can make fording the creek hazardous.

La Verkin Creek is the principal drainage in the Kolob section of the park. It and its tributaries have sliced amazing canyons into the deep red Navajo sandstone formation. Numerous small springs supplement La Verkin Creek, especially from Gregory Butte to the Willis/La Verkin Creek confluence.

Vegetation ranges from dry sage flats to mossy deciduous and conifer forest. Hanging gardens drape seepage areas. Cottonwoods shade the river bottom where the canyon is wider; pinyon pine and juniper anchor the talus slopes above.

Hiking destinations include the small cascade and pools downstream from the "Corral," Willis Creek, Hop Valley, and Kolob Arch. Officially measured at 310 feet, Kolob Arch may be the largest free-standing arch in the world. Other small canyons invite exploration — the time spent is well worth it.

To reach the trailhead from the Kolob Canyons Visitor Center, head east on the Kolob Canyons Road 3.5 miles to Lee Pass.

The trail loses elevation for 1.2 miles until it reaches Timber Creek (may be dry in late summer.) After following Timber Creek for more than 1.5 miles, the trail climbs for .5 mile then begins a long descent into La Verkin Creek. The trail meets the creek near the historic "Corral" shown on the topographic map, and is fairly level as it heads up the valley on the north side of the creek to the Kolob Arch Trail Junction.

The trail to the Kolob Arch Viewpoint parallels a tiny creek, dropping into the wash and winding among the boulders to the confluence of three small drainages. Note that the trail climbs up onto a tree-covered bench. Look Up! Kolob Arch is about 1/4 mile away, high on the cliffs above. This is the end of the trail. Please prevent erosion by staying off the unstable slopes.

Continuing up La Verkin Creek from Kolob Arch Trail Junction, the trail soon fords the stream — the crossing is usually shallow. There is a reliable spring to the right across the creek. Uphill a short way is the Hop Valley Trail Junction (p. 36.)

The La Verkin Creek Canyon begins to narrow near Beartrap Canyon. Stream fordings become frequent; you may get your feet wet. The trail is not clearly defined from this area upstream; choose what looks like the most direct route.

Kolob Arch from the end of the trail.

This trail section ends at delightful Beartrap Canyon. See pages 42-44 for more on Beartrap, or if you wish to continue up La Verkin and Willis Creeks.

See pages 42-44

Camping   Camping is not permitted from Lee Pass to south of Shuntavi Butte. There are numerous popular campsites along the rest of this hike, regulated by Park Service use zones. In certain areas, camping has compacted the soils and altered the natural scene — the "corral" area; some areas within ¼ mile of Kolob Arch Trail Junction; and areas near the river ford downstream from the Hop Valley Trail Junction. Camping is not prohibited in these areas, but for the health of your backcountry and to prevent further regulation, consider camping in other areas. Avoid both heavily used and pristine spots; slightly used sites, out of sight of the trail, are recommended. Avoid damaging any vegetation.

Areas below the high water line may be used during low flash flood threat periods. Additional camp areas are found downstream from the "Corral," on the south side of La Verkin Creek (opposite the trail) and upstream from the Hop Valley Trail Junction.

If you enter this area from Lee Pass, you must get your backcountry permit at the Kolob Canyons Visitor Center where additional information is provided.

A coachwhip.